DADDY'S LITTLE GIRL

By De Vida Gill

Illustrated by Kevin Gentry

DADDY'S LITTLE GIRL

Attention: Permissions Department
Diverse Child
2913 El Camino Real, #129
Tustin, CA 92782

ISBN# 978-0-9850028-6-2
Printed in the United States of America

Written by De Vida Gill
Illustrated by Kevin Gentry

This SPECIAL EDITION poetry in motion book
is dedicated to my Daddy
Dr. Russell V. Gill
1942 - 2019

Some call him Mister while others
call him Sir
but Daddy is the name that I prefer.

With a smile on his face
and sparkle in his eye

he's wrapped around my little
finger like a bright pink bow tie.

The music plays loud as
I dance on his shoes.
He hugs and laughs
while singing the blues.

Jazz and gospel and oldies surround
but there's nothing quite like sharing
that ole' Motown sound.

Tug-a-war with licorice,
watching movies galore,

stories in the moonlight,
dropping popcorn on the floor.

My Daddy, My HERO with a big "D" on his chest

protects and provides
for his family and pets.

He leads by example
knowledge and wisdom to be shared

my Daddy
is a genius

and I AM his heir;

not the Queen but the Princess…

spoiled… Oh, No!

Just well taken care of with a big bright pink bow.

DR. DE VIDA GILL is a Licensed Clinical Social Worker and Certified Transformational Coach/Strategist. She has touched numerous lives from children to adults by creating opportunities to embrace and celebrate their authentic selves by integrating arts/entertainment, mental health and education. In addition to her diverse writing projects and philanthropic engagement, Dr. Gill is an active member of Alpha Kappa Alpha Sorority, Inc. For more information, visit diversechild.com.

Other Children's Books by Dr. De Vida Gill:

For more information, visit Diversechild.com

Made in the USA
Columbia, SC
18 February 2020